GRAVITY

WELL

RESCUE PRESS

CHICAGO | CLEVELAND | IOWA CITY

Design by Sevy Perez
ITC Avant Garde & Adobe Caslon Pro
rescuepress.co

GRAVITY

WELL

MARC

RAHE

for Leigh

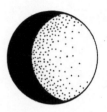

WAXING CRESCENT

WAXING GIBBOUS

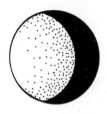

WANING GIBBOUS

WANING CRESCENT

The Size of Me

I was the size of a flower, many
different sizes. The time of year factored.

Rainfall. Cloud cover. I was one size when
a bee entered. When a bee entered, I held

a narrative in a moment. Moment:
a link in a chain, chain dropped in

a bucket of chains, links touching many
links. There was sunshine and a history of

protein chains. To evolve was the general
purpose, but to let sunlight grow me in

soil was the purpose. Pollen attaches
to a fuzzy body drawn to nectar.

To re-tell the narrative changes the narrative
is the story. To the advantage

of tiny hook-like appendages, I
have no smooth surface.

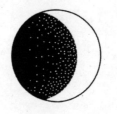

Election Cycle

The morning sun is beautiful. Its light,
I mean, reflected from the leaves about

to fall and the blood fresh beneath our mouths,
and here is a crow undoing a Hefty bag.

Over there is a birdhouse
near a birdfeeder in a lawn we own,

if *paying for* means that, and we have,
in our heart, enacted caring

in the exchange of paper and metal
money for a bag of seed

we'll never lay before anyone we love
that has the words *thank you*,

uncommon in the speech of birds.
We made the house with tools and hands

we would describe as our own, if.

Writer Friend

Writing, trying to remember
what a Marc Rahe poem sounds like
in a forecast-come-true afternoon
of cloudy and scattered, I
opened your book for encouragement
to the one with the cinderblock.

Again I wish we'd known each
other as high school friends, maybe
worked afternoons or weekends together.
Not all the time to talk, but some
between separate or shared tasks
that were, or could have been, good

practice for the tasks to come.
The image in this poem could be you
in a shirt with matching cap, standing
next to your parents' car in a driveway.
The sun is clearly setting, or has recently,
but your colors are still brilliant in the flash.

Never to Divide by Zero

A voice raised in anger at the office,
raised and sustained. Someone's job
is to watch for the light of past events
in the sky. Eyes and antennae raised
in hindsight. What would you rather
undertake as part of your last day?
With prescription sunglasses
and a functional player

one can subdue miles, lot
after lot containing second
stomachs. What is the value
of a dollar rejected by a machine?
Above, butterflies and raptors
lend their wings to gargoyles.

Host

Did I forget to lock up on the way out?
This then that of the lobby is revealed
as shadows evade sunlight permitted
entry by the glass in the facade of this
edifice, the structure wherein my labors
and hours earn for me compensation.

A living. The city is never ready enough
for the populace and guests readying
for the home game. Unusual hours

made usual by virtue of ritual. Tradition.
To time-honor. To excuse. Libation.
Liberation. Lip service. The sun cuts

its arc from the sky, never has to do a thing.

Belong and Resist Belonging

Hands around a face.

One hand scolds the others,
their *different length*, their

so slow. That hand speaking
at the speed of seconds, loud
voice hollow as a hall.

My cough again. The same
waking kills sleep again

for the day's nourishment.
Hot breakfast. Cold breakfast.

Scarf holds my breath awhile
but the air takes it away

for the sky, for anybody. Above,
the few dark leaves stir, remain.

Our Shared Life

The bee trapped
with you inside

your helmet in traffic,
will or will not.

You had a bad
dream once where your

parents never let
you win at anything,

woke, crawled in with.

Today is overcast.
After too much

coffee, you are
hard to bear. Claws

of a fowl break
water's surface,

make a river
graceful with landing.

Previous Lives

Stacked waist-high along the wall of the grimy
and cobwebbed dining room—a ceiling fan,
but the curtains drawn last when?—were calendars.
Expired. Square days x-ed away and square
days whiter than hair, whiter than cataracts.

There was ongoing, then over. Bare feet,
then the relief of stepping from cold tile
to the kitchen rug. From cold tile
to the bathroom rug, the cold of rubbing
alcohol applied to open skin. The question of
that day of the dog's bath—whose first memory?

Rumination: a stack of squares. Beads off
the string, the ones never retrieved down the vent
in the dark and mildew of the duct works.
What is before the breath, what after?
How could anyone sleep so close to the tracks?

The same stars above. Water from the tap
beside. There is only so much
between the lines of an equal sign.
The lines never meeting, parallel, containing space
but open, like this house revisited,
windows all open now to draw air,
to disturb the mess, ruin ruins.

First Frost

It's the familiarity
you notice first, a feeling not gotten
over, but put away. Again you're surprised
how a sweater gets that smell, boxed so long.

When the leaves began to turn,
you thought of the rake, started
putting it off early, maybe
get to it on time this year.

You find a walnut wedged in
the crack of a path stone. When
getting up gets harder, you remind

yourself these days are temporary.
You watch the weather most nights,
remembering the losses, the near misses.

Unwashed

Sound of tap water impenetrable
to the phone ring, you are a compartment
in which I focus. In which cleaning

the remaining paste from my utensils
doesn't entail any tearing at my ear
but for your tear. But for my part

I am amazed at how you, a noise,
form a portal in that part of the total
where the motions of these hands make

from many things, one task, apart;
under your canopy I hone my use.

Crossing the Street

The cold brings blood to the child's cheek.
He makes his way through the morning
to school. The scarf wet before his mouth.

Through the light snow cover, the cement
is revealed where he's stepped. What can be seen
looking behind. An animal may not be dead in the street.

Memory is the predawn ceiling
seen through the blanket. Memory is
the almost-forgotten hug before leaving.

Going ahead is to find out. A hand for the door,
redness to fade in the warmth. Warmth
to fade, despite the working limbs, in the recess.

On Sleeping Well

She's still asleep so I take my coffee to the farthest room. There are new webs I'll need to remove, silver in the sunbeam at the hinge edge of the door. I clear space on the desk; stacks of books like neglected friends, all facing the same way. I'm reading an astronaut's memoir. One must have to like the learning to train repeatedly for unlikely contingencies. In the slant-light, shadows of frost across the carpet. Strange to say *at the mercy of* weather conditions. To ask—knowing only what you knew then, would you make the same decisions? I've thought this morning (a dozen times?) *a faint vinegar now I've cleaned the urn.* Through a strand, vibration calls a spider to the struggle.

Open Enrollment

Become the mechanic of our shared space.
This is a cart with mixed parts.
In the eyes of the heart

of the earth, we will always be those that
must be drawn nearer. We needn't select
agreement to proceed. What is missing,
if anything, when you stand under

a white sky on a bridge, from the sound
of a fowl landing on river?

Birthday

The numbness was explained to me
in my fingers. Downriver
from the forest in my neck.

A smaller and smaller forest.
Branches always closer.

Though I could still grip
my arthritic grip, bring
the cup with both hands.

In that time, my job had light lifting.
For the successor I left notes, passwords
on one Post-It. I tried to be helpful,

but we never know. To look for change
in my pockets meant having to look.

Surface Tension

The cat sleeps now
on the towel on the floor
in the corner between
the wall and the bathtub.

So precisely in place.
White cat. Green towel.

While the cat sleeps,
his side rises, slowly.
The cat scratched me once
when I was petting him.

He was prepared
to define a limit,
like a line drawn,
or a level of milk
risen to, or just past,
its vessel's brim.

Nightstand

Ground divorces from ground and red from the heart
beneath the press that screws, with love, the apple
toward cider. Fragments are left of spectrum
when chlorophyll abandons the leaves, old

yellowing story. Selling dismisses
picking. A classic of skyrocketed
afternoon becomes lewd, interpreted.
Her favorite song from childhood dragged

through bong water by black light. Midnight, you
held me once through the lace veil interrupted
by actual touch. What made a recipe for
vinegar of if/then, therefore N or

negative N. Sum or its homonym.
Both cuffs are open beside the water.

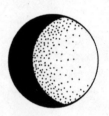

Where All Motes Lead

All day the wooden sphere gets
thought of as *tilted on its axis*.
Day and night the sphere gets
defined *globe* by its mapped-on
surface, darkened with age.

The angle of the axis
to the horizontal ornament stand
defines an arc. It suggests
an open mouth or a raised arm.

There is a pen holder, too, though
the pen is years ago lost. The cup
of the holder even now angles
up in welcome. Or is the holder
meant to suggest a telescope?

At one careful distance
from every edge, the sphere keeps
its heart at its center.

Night and day there is no sun,
no terminus any part of the surface
moves toward. The sphere is still.

Turning Forty

The day I turned

my wheelchair onto my street

in a downpour, the calendar
became more personal.

That white collection and
occasional calligraphic

erotic entry—I'll
never forget the time

I reread the Dickinson
with the fly

descending my

glass (itself an
occasion

of condensation)

on the table
to my friends
before the toast
to all my friends

and our time
together

permanently now
in the past
bound.

Monument

These check stubs are marked and perforated
foreshadowings of our regret. Bottomless
is the cup of our addiction before the slots,
as the curtains insist the nature of aspiration
exposed in our regard for wavelength, and what
powers the recoil of the lever, the raven relieving
itself as it takes flight from the tombstone?

Your neurons await the blackout and recollect
clammy innocence reenacted
when put drunk into the taxi, polished
and chromatic like nails against the palm;
a leafless tree cut loose from context,
roots and branches reduced in analogy
to what serves to be like for other; promise.

Design Specifications

I provide a snack, three machines,
a movie I found with the color orange
repeated to music in scenes. She asks

for a blanket, zips her sweater chin-ward.
When I push the thing on the thermostat,
the counter-thing needles redly up

the number line. We don't know where we are
connected or in how many places.
At the edge of the bookshelf an action

figure sits in one of its five postures.
We learned sharing and cooperation
just being around. I point a device
at a device and know which button.

Appetite

Earth's shadow fakes a smile with the moon.
Headlights shadow a field of stalks away
over snow. My own shadow shadows me.
I am allowed,

sometimes, by my house not far from its shelter.
What I've had to eat teases my hunger to come
again. For more is what I'm made.

I've been reopened along the same incision
and though metal plates and wires, metal screws,
can only be said to ache, I say
it is the metal in this leg that tells me
the sky is so full of mountains and trenches
as the ocean, metal that warns me
of my own weight held past a certain angle from the center.

But anyone made, roasting these potatoes until they're
about right, might turn the calendar to the next scene—
a new sky over a different shore, with windowed
structures in the foreground and white sails
demonstrating distance—might lift the reminder-squares
to face the wall, raise that hole to the nail.

Inhuman

I will fall asleep but wake with the same
mind. There was a boot print dirt
patterned on a jacket I found at a bargain.
I would like to become so eloquent.

There is much diction beyond me;
admissible details in the kitchen
fixtures. Features. Geese
in formation lower toward the river

to follow, but then not to land. Is parallel
what those reflections are?
It's the quality of vision—flicker
fusion threshold—that enables

the hawk to strike at that speed,
how the frames need to advance
only so fast for the illusion.

August Keeps Its Promise

The air is as wet as dog's breath; sweat reverse-tears
into the eye. The shirt weighs needier step by step,
clinging. With each step, the self-consciousness rises;
the cloud of ugliness cartoons over my head, neon
lightning pointing to my body for pedestrian
edification: be not this man. August keeps its promise,

steep with degrees. All I want is a drink, and I'm not
giving it to me. No one insists anything to me
but they all steam away as I pass. Only the river
risks my attention, glinting. At crosswalks,
drivers seem unlicensed, out of state.
I watch my feet more. On the sidewalk there—
a worn sticker depicting the Bat-Signal.

Fable of the Cephalopod

I coughed and coughed and coughed.

I coughed up an ocean of sea monsters.

I coughed up an octopus that was trying to wear a sweater.
This sweater was made of another, grumpier octopus.
That octopus was so grumpy, he kicked off his boot.

It's still in there, that boot, so near my heart; familiar to me now,
I hear it barking up the wrong bronchial tree.

Ice Cubes against the Glass

Making my own inner darkness smaller
with its volume, my liver hangs.

Its functions black and white
with color illustrations, but decades

ago. That room was hot all semester,
all of us in. But we learned

by going where we had to go.
The radiator pinged loudly, lest

we forget. I forget all the functions
but see spots here and there

where a refresher wouldn't hurt,
as teacher would say.

Goodbye by goodbye, she, then I,
wave as if in greeting.

State Park

Moss on a wooden bench. Often a shadow
passes, or a cloudless hour.
These figures meet—a woman and a dog,
a man who smiles and a boy shy to pet.

Voices cross and rise from the lake.
Pine needles on the bacterial floor
soften the sound. It is cooler there.
White sails over white boats distant

enough to hide more than one with a thumb.
A dog on its side down in the wood chips,
"running" like a stooge. Does it itch?
Then up and off, tongue to the wind that carries

the news, pieces of tree in the hair.
Exposed on the path: some roots, a stone.

The Sky without Air

You may be linked by fingers
in the kingdom of the blind.
On your shoulder is a hand.
You give one hand to the body
before you. What is a passerby
but a sound? But even litter
shouts of the wind. Your one
hand unoccupied, what do

you do with freedom? The same
heels always in your path.

How to Use a Gravity Well as a Slingshot

Color-coded flags in the yard where not to dig.
Someone knocks, stands awhile. Gives up,

goes away. Things I'm going to fix include
a bite, involve adding elements of fire and water.

In the night the sound of something outside
I wish would die faster.

Floor Plan

I've seen the floor plan of this place:
the second floor of the library.
Walking from the elevator to the stacks
then to this table—just big enough
for two seated facing each other,
though I'm alone, a low partition
between—I saw three individuals
at separate tables and a group of three.
The woman in a striped shirt looked
at me, unsmiling. No one else looked
at me that I saw.

It's easy to imagine seven small blue x-es
on the second-floor floor plan
and the spaces around and between them
organized by their presence. Though
we walk rather than plummet,
last night I heard explained
that one BB surrounded by a baseball stadium
hints at the vastness between
the atomic nucleus and its electron shell
by a voice from speakers
set apart from the image on the screen.

In Winter

The melting snow reveals the tunnel
made by a field mouse
withholding its body from the sky's
predations—

from the shifting grays of sky—
from the beguiling many-whited sky.

As the white of the sky becomes
the white of the cold-forgiving
ground, so dies the field mouse:

not embraced by but impaled on
one crystalline arm
of death's symmetrical body.

Stellar

Above the hill the recently releafed dome gives testimony of the sun. The bell rings the pedestrians still in their day clothes to their destinations. The open mouth of the bell and the traffic sounds make use in the open air.

These wide lawns of the state are well tended, many storied, a small chore to climb.

Remember that August? The shade shifted away while you slept. Your book and sandals in the grass. How tender you were after dinner, to the touch.

How much of what in you was being used up those manic days? A wind of words, and behind each word a collision of this then that notion. What escaped only hinted at its birth.

This tree was my favorite the day it rained during my walk. Uncanny when it's raining and it's sunny at the same time. As if being in someone's presence and feeling the presence of their ghost.

When we return to the graveyard to drive past the statue and the wind in petals and flags, we always recognize something new. "Look: someone has painted the sign." Yellow glistens in the letters and digits.

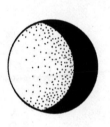

Observatory

Morning is an ancient thing in motion.
Were they like us, the primal, self-aware

stargazers? All day the veil blue or gray.
All day certain scintillating beauty

and inexhaustible darkness withheld
from us. From us comes the want. Earth, turn me.

Let Me Say This

Let me say this washing machine
is a well, its shadowed interior

deepening to the black wet.
My mother's in there, and the tiny

child-me digging to China, falling
from the tree, cringing at the dog's

voluminous shout. Let me say it
because she was always with

a garden hose or at the sink.
I would say "Playing in water again"

again and again while she worked
and wore down. Or let me say eroded,

washed away, diminished, then gone,
but someplace. Let me say it,

and let me listen
through the hollow.

Blackout

In which you become third person to yourself,
one unable to see the snow for the snow.

In which a pole makes the compass meaningless.
In which down is that which weighs all things

toward itself. Meanwhile, a grackle takes a beetle
in the garden. Inside the heart, the tree is pierced

by letters, and whether the wind rattles branches
or forces green leaves to the grass made wet

by condensate which sparkles and awaits
a change, the arrow is time regardless.

Still you make the eggs, discard the shells
in the disposal. You run the water a little longer.

How I Miss You

One block of street hosts a rough ride:
imported bricks from across the river.

The river a natural border. We are not
alone, alone. Your bricks are brought in,

hard to drive in winter. To get home.
What is warmth without your arm on me?

This is your street your numbers bring
my letters to, like a spell. Of summoning.

In summoning is a sound like in love.
In love, my words are a tree in winter—

leafless, under a low sky, in an afternoon,
in a field covered in white.

The Bumblebee

One, just flying into a flower of the zucchini plant as
I approach the garden. It is cooler this morning, and the
prickles of the leaves have dew. I try to give the bee space as I
pass through the narrow between the plants. I can hear the buzz
those wings make. The bee flies to another plant.
Behind me, the door is closed. Several birds fly away.
When I pick the only ripe cherry tomato, possibly the same
bee flies from beneath a near leaf. I'm not hurt.

Attic

I am forgetful, but one has pressed flowers

in a directory. How I know
is I discovered them later,

years later judging
by the receipt used as a marker.

One other thing is a jacket marked
"Flight Surgeon" with her earring

in a pocket. Up in a blue daydream,
beauty weighs the mystery of her implied ear.

And how, with war released from the blades,
the blades cut such a figure of sky.

Still a wasp nest could be inscribed with prohibition
of fear, a calm that sits to the side. A stillness

through which the storm can be imagined
to watch. An attractive weed

can be discerned to persist
across the grounds.

In Gratitude

I'm itchy now I disturbed a stillness.
The stillness had been at once
at a level and accumulating:
a self-construction
of unused pieces of time
and subtle matter. Beneath it all

was your book.
Though the stillness
had become
a rain made of void,
and did hang of itself
independently in the void,
though the stillness was alone
and entire,
I had another desire:
to re-read your book.

I have become itchy,
the result of the self-defense of stillness.
But—

I have now
what I wanted
then. I am not sorry.

Winter Bed

Your body is still while you dream.
Your murmur, audible to the conscious,
is the wake behind the vessel of your dreaming.

Without mood, the sunlight moves
across the floor. Counting lets me
give myself a face for waiting.

Breath. Breath. Minutes run in place
in red. Mostly covered, I could still
drink the cold water. The weight

of cover is a place. I will see the fresh snow
already contains animal tracks.
Beneath the snow, the sidewalk leads away.

On Seasons

A button which once was reserved, now
undone slowly left
out in the gravity.
Like a belt of stars
unfastened, like a fist
of stone felled by caress.

Natural light. Kitchen smells.

When more than two mouths
are to be fed after silently
mouthing the prayer,
the organ's flesh
hangs in flesh to open.
A waft, then memory's bent knuckle.

Thankful

I was thankful for opportunity
but, lacking, I awaited the loss
of my means. I examined

my lacking and dwelled
on it. I held my lacking in

mind like a light I could breathe
and freeze. I took the heat
from my lacking and sculpted

the remains of lacking,
what was left inside me.

I made eagle wings, a stairway,
seven stars in the shape
of a dragon from a tale

of dragon's devotion
to maiden. I sculpted

from lacking a devastation
of the land and the development
of a fountain of blight.

Therein, a bleak foundation;
it was a pale light.

Without, the heat: soft frenzy
dispersing my devisable breath.

One Girl

The full moon in March is the Full Worm Moon.
A week later, it is afternoon uphill
from the river that runs through
campus. Between edifices, a frisbee
has been brought into the rare warm air

by boys and a girl. As I pass,
I hear behind me a boy stumble
after a missed catch. The hollow
sound of frisbee scraping sidewalk.
In short sleeves, I am almost sweating.

The Organ

The lid slides inaudibly open.
Microcosm adjusts in the lashes,
accustomed to making do. Light makes
its determined way through the pupil.
What it carries in its frequencies
enters cells and ends.
Then a process is begun.

The organ floats in the dark.
The organ is not motionless
or patient. Other, inner,
variables are moving side to side
in equations. The remainder is kept

and I am the keeper,
earnest or negligent.
Things go, one could say, regardless.
I nod. I am in case.
Behind the business of the organ,
there is a quiet space I can fit.
I nod and drowse.

Even the light-corpse
floats in its jar, though
the jar is close to the shelf edge
high above a rotting floor.

I Slept

I slept like a baby.

I slept like a log.

I slept like a forest

of baby logs
and feel much

better this morning.
With some milk

and a wood chisel
you could coax

the you from my slumber.

Black Morning

In the black morning-before-morning
sleep lies like scattered bricks.

Inside the black between the bricks
the word *no* sparks, shivering
against itself. In the interior of even
one brick is a table where
a prayer can never be finished
over the white dishes and white
cloth where already
purple and brown stains appear
while nearby the lonely and the dead
teach lessons on patience.

The interior surface of the brick
is as green as a minute.

Is Coincidence a Spring of Romance

If one turns from the shelf
and hears "I'm reading that, too,"
that is a signal of intention from the universe.
A glimmer of *how remarkable*
and *was meant to be.*

And what a conversation piece!
Or consider dumb luck.
What lands in our lap may have been best
gone whizzing past. Spring sprung:
a watch twice daily right.

Stay

Snowmelt refreezes
in the shadow the house

casts on the walk.
Late afternoon

recommends a sleep, tucks
me away in my rooms.

A book wakes me as I
drop it falling asleep.

A system generates pain
in my head. The clock keeps

pulling the future down.
At a point, the phone moves

in place; its offer
continues awhile.

Scar Tissue

Rain began above while we were unaware.
Humid for days; we felt like we'd done a wrong.

Our pores opened: mechanical, utilitarian.
We went inside the library. Call numbers

lashed spines to a system. Through the wall
of a study room, laughter could be

described as braying. Once at a blood draw
my vein resisted the needle. The needle

slipped aside inside my arm, despite
repeated attempts. I made,

for the phlebotomist, a joke I hoped
would defuse her growing anxiety.

I waited for her smile in the white. Outside
the library, a black metal table

on a small patio in the embrace of three
brick walls sits empty. I could sit there too.

Not Yet

Neither the oil under the black
plastic cap of the vial
nor the flower that yielded

is the scent that still rises
days after you've left
the pillow.

With breath to draw scent
within breath, scent comes alive
with each breath and time

bends me in memory to you.
If to wake is to leave,
then sleep. In memory

your small sounds in the dark
close enough distance;
your knuckles against my palm
spell some word I could learn.

Something Else

Gray and darker gray tail feathers held
against the wood of a high corner
of my privacy fence—the mourning dove

has nested again this season. Twigs
and something blue in there make home enough.
During a heat wave last year, I thought

she would die. Looking from my kitchen,
air from the vent gave me gooseflesh.
The passing of time rewarded me:

a feeling of relief, the beauty,
a chick where none had been.
She can be still in the rain, too.

Funeral Rose

I clumsily touch
with my twisted joints
and bones. These two
fingers like a satyr's legs
in a natural dance
on your garden.

Tonight it will not snow
despite the season's usual desire.
This afternoon fog hid
the sky and the lake and the shore.
Only the solid line of the bridge
was visible—a guide
from a story of the underworld.

How could my spirit rest
in a coffin with my head
so lonely on that cushion?
Possessing nothing
but a strength born of urgency,
how could my spirit become
a horn to sound its sigh-less
position, or a horn to pry
a lid, to lift it
like a leg?

Alumni Weekend

Despite the past the tree is still
greening this April Sunday, the river now
calm and marking its course.

Students with packs pass the tree,
cross the river. The parking lot
is mostly empty today by the tree.

No one is leaning against the tree
where we leaned and kissed
and you hinted. We lit our shadows

with the same cigarette your lipstick
made another faint kiss around.
One man crosses the lot briskly

from building to car. I imagine
him counting his steps, to share
the sum, over dinner, with his wife.

Appliances

Blue above, your sunlight lights the white
in this snow but leaves it crystalline.

Tomorrow's flood is poised, but
here is a frozen pipe. And here

is my electric oven providing me
with more opportunity to practice.

Blue sky, you are clear out there
in the polar beyond my door.

Through glass I see you.
And here is a bucket of sand.

With the handle fully turned
there is a constant trickle.

The Fluorescent Bulb

will last for years.
As it reminds you
in a tight, constant

whine each time it's on.
"That's all you're going
to do?" a former

roommate remarked
once and every time
I don't finish

the dishes ever since.
Every workday waiting
for or rushing to

the bus, I'm as
alive as I'm
ever going to be

except as echoes
living in
your smallest bones.

The Centipede

for Jason Bradford

The centipede crawls over the tissue
in my wastebasket. I've seen her
or a similar other
in my bathtub recently. Perhaps she
is an admiral. Perhaps this
is an inspection, as though
the garbage is my vessel. Several
microscopic white gloves,
the indiscernible truth of them,
reveal to her how I'm doing. I feel
gratitude. A little afraid,
responsible, I raise my hand.

Pale Coat

Here where you show me your old ink
between two rivers, a cat sleeps in the drive
with knowledge revealed by the parting
orchard grass split by the surreptitious passing

of a field mouse. Many bees get on one
fallen apple; a sour smell come up
from its open skin, makes a swarm of its own
in the light that heats and rises even

in the shady rows. Bites welt and constellate
our skin. We are chemical beacons beholden
to the same sky clouded with primer; grind
our resentments beneath the toxic blanket.

See the shadow on the lot. Shadow darkens,
focuses a false bird before the strike.

Finals

The clipped rattle of ventilation
and fluorescent gnaw audibly; judge
your anxiety and attention in the cubicle
where learning is the struggle between
this exhaustion and those procrastinations.

There is a word for the way odor flowers
from the carpet, rises and makes a show
of the indefatigability of what grows
in the decimal system called darkness
and you know something is back

there, traced black in motion that spasms
like a grandparent stretched against the white:
a word of primal, forgotten urgency behind
the sheet before you if, in time, you can see it.

Because

the bush is pretty but knocks against
my bedroom window.

Seed dropped
there by wind or animal in the crack.

A small crack between foundation
and walk, but enough.

Leaves
fanned on slender branches
like an arrangement or plumage.

I yelled a little one night, mistaking
in my sleep the sound waking
me was at my bedroom door.

The shadow of the bush
through my window, across the floor,
swayed.

Alone, I was still
deeply embarrassed. Though the swaying
left no mark or texture of vein

there was no consolation in its shape.

Option

Stars that didn't
move correctly were
called wanderers,
planets. Water exists
on some of them, too,
and rain that isn't water,
elsewhere. Beneath our
oceans are vents. Mineral-
rich bubbles rise
from the boil of the molten
center, and a life.

Nostalgia

Sitting there bare-assed on the formerly thrift-priced
couch in the shared living room—a private space
for another forty or so minutes—your lipstick
left its evidence on the glass rim made artifact

by nostalgia. Wonder. Like the moment
you made that soft gesture with your cheek
against that part of my cerebellum that lights
up in the magnetic coffin. So tight

a space in the motionless white where motion
is never far from whatever the mind is.
If only a poster could be before me
in the clinical machine, I would have it be

the map of who you were to me in my mind
then in the now that fades like life.

To Live in Interesting Times

The fluorescent light seems to struggle
against death. Not dead yet, the fixture
pulses every few or several seconds,
bequeathing humility to the shadows.

The light is beacon-like above the shelves
of biography—the book named *Elon Musk*,
the book named *Flannery O'Connor*.
Not being people, the biographies seem

un-irritated, self-contained. I am so
irritated I can barely contain myself.
I have "practis'd so long to learn to read,"
but now feel myself as attention launched against

that light. Someone is responsible.
I am just a patron of this library.

Acknowledgments

Thank you to Patrick Flanagan, Melissa Ginsburg, Rebecca Lehmann, and Niki Neems for your support and guidance.

My continuing gratitude to Danny Khalastchi, Caryl Pagel, Sevy Perez, Alyssa Perry, and the rest of the team at Rescue Press.

Sincere thanks to the editors and staff of the following publications. Some poems appeared in different versions.

The Iowa Review: "Nightstand" and "Scar Tissue"

The Journal Petra: "Election Cycle," "Funeral Rose," "Inhuman," and "Thankful"

MAKE Literary Magazine: "Never to Divide by Zero," "One Girl," "On Seasons," and "The Sky without Air"

Pangyrus: "To Live in Interesting Times"

MARC RAHE is the author of *The Smaller Half* (Rescue Press, 2010), *On Hours* (Rescue Press, 2015), and *Gravity Well* (Rescue Press, 2020). His poems have appeared in *The Iowa Review*, *jubilat*, *MAKE Literary Magazine*, *PEN Poetry Series*, *Sixth Finch*, and other literary journals. He lives in Iowa City.